アメリカ合衆国建国の父

ジョージ・ワシントンの霊言

SPIRITUAL INTERVIEW
with
GEORGE WASHINGTON

大川隆法
RYUHO OKAWA

本霊言は、2016年9月22日、幸福の科学 特別説法堂にて、公開収録された（写真上・下）。

アメリカ合衆国建国の父
ジョージ・ワシントンの霊言

Spiritual Interview with
George Washington

Preface

Today, American people are apt to think too small. Please remember the good old days and think about America's Founding Father, "George Washington." Now is the day to rebuild the United States.

"Think Big" and restart the movement toward "Greater America."

This book is the true Spiritual Interview with George Washington. You'd easily find the fountain of new wisdom.

This is the voice of God in disguise.

Please believe your new hope and future.

Oct. 11th, 2016
Master Ryuho Okawa

はじめに

　今日、アメリカの人々は考え方が小さくなってきたようだ。どうか、楽しかった昔の日々を思い出し、アメリカ建国の父「ジョージ・ワシントン」に思いを馳せてほしい。

　今こそ、合衆国再建の時なのだ。

　「大きく考え」、「より偉大なアメリカ」づくりを再スタートさせよう。

　本書は、ジョージ・ワシントンの本物の霊言である。ページをめくれば、知恵の泉がこんこんと湧き出してくることだろう。

　これが姿を変えた神の声でもあるのだ。

　あなたがたには新しい希望と未来が待っていることを、どうか信じてほしい。

2016 年 10 月 11 日
あなたがたの師　大川隆法

Contents

Preface 2

1 America's Founding Father Washington Appears 12

2 In the American Presidential Election, He Supports the "Honest Man" 20

3 On Racial Problems in Current America 36

4 He Helped God Make a New Civilization 48

5 On America's Foreign Policies on the Middle East and Russia 54

6 On American and World Economies 58

7 On Problems with North Korea 66

8 The Secret of the God of America 74

9 His Past Lives as a God in India, Europe, and Africa 86

10 Declaring His Rebirth as Donald Trump 92

* This spiritual interview was conducted in English. The Japanese text is a translation added by the Happy Science International Editorial Division.

目　次

はじめに ……………………………………………………… 3

1　「アメリカ建国の父」ワシントン登場 …………………… 13

2　米大統領選では、あの「正直者」を応援 ………………… 21

3　現代アメリカの人種問題について ………………………… 37

4　神が新文明を拓くのを手伝った …………………………… 49

5　米国の中東・ロシア外交について ………………………… 55

6　アメリカ経済と世界経済について ………………………… 59

7　北朝鮮問題について ………………………………………… 67

8　「アメリカの神」の秘密 …………………………………… 75

9　過去世はインド、ヨーロッパ、アフリカの神 …………… 87

10　ドナルド・トランプとしての転生を明言 ……………… 93

※本書は、英語で収録された霊言に和訳を付けたものです。

This book is the transcript of spiritual messages given by George Washington.

These spiritual messages were channeled through Ryuho Okawa. However, please note that because of his high level of enlightenment, his way of receiving spiritual messages is fundamentally different from other psychic mediums who undergo trances and are completely taken over by the spirits they are channeling.

It should be noted that these spiritual messages are opinions of the individual spirits and may contradict the ideas or teachings of the Happy Science Group.

本書は、ジョージ・ワシントンの霊言を収録したものである。

　「霊言現象」とは、あの世の霊存在の言葉を語り下ろす現象のことをいう。これは高度な悟りを開いた者に特有のものであり、「霊媒現象」（トランス状態になって意識を失い、霊が一方的にしゃべる現象）とは異なる。

　ただ、「霊言」は、あくまでも霊人の意見であり、幸福の科学グループとしての見解と矛盾する内容を含む場合がある点、付記しておきたい。

Spiritual Interview with George Washington

September 22, 2016
Special Lecture Hall, Happy Science
Spiritual Messages from George Washington

アメリカ合衆国建国の父
ジョージ・ワシントンの霊言

2016年9月22日　幸福の科学 特別説法堂にて
ジョージ・ワシントンの霊言

George Washington (1732-1799)

An American military official and politician. He was born as a child of a plantation owner and he, himself, gained great wealth through managing the plantation. He grew to fame as the commander of the British colony military fighting for the French in the French and Indian War in 1775. After the Battles of Lexington and Concord in 1775, he was appointed as commander-in-chief by the Continental Army and fought for American independence. After his resignation from commander-in-chief, he was elected as the president of the constitutional convention. Through the first American presidential election in 1789, he was elected as the first president and laid the foundation of the federal system. He came to be called America's "founding father," his portrait is now printed on the dollar bill, and his name is now used for the capital, an aircraft carrier, and a university.

Interviewers from Happy Science

Masayuki Isono

>Executive Director, Chief of Overseas Missionary Work Promotion Office, Deputy Chief Secretary, First Secretarial Division Religious Affairs Headquarters

Yuta Okawa

>Managing Director, Deputy Chief of CEO's Office Religious Affairs Headquarters, Advisor of General Headquarters, Activity Promotion Strategist of Political Headquarters, Activity Promotion Strategist of International Headquarters

Shugaku Tsuiki

>Executive Director, President of Happy Science Institute of Government and Management

※ Interviewers are listed in the order that they appear in the transcript. The professional titles represent the position at the time of the interview.

ジョージ・ワシントン（1732 － 1799）

アメリカ合衆国の軍人、政治家。農園経営者の子として生まれ、自身も大規模な農園経営により富を築いた。1755 年、イギリス植民地軍の司令官としてフレンチ・インディアン戦争で仏軍側と戦い、名を上げる。1775 年のレキシントン・コンコードの戦い後、大陸会議にて大陸軍の総司令官に任命され、アメリカ独立戦争を戦う。総司令官辞任後は憲法制定議会の議長に選出。1789 年、最初のアメリカ合衆国大統領選挙で初代大統領に選ばれ、連邦制の基礎を築いた。「アメリカ合衆国建国の父」と呼ばれ、現在も肖像画が紙幣に用いられ、首都、空母、大学等の名称にその名が使われている。

質問者（幸福の科学）

磯野将之（理事　兼　宗務本部海外伝道推進室長　兼　第一秘書局担当局長）

大川裕太（常務理事　兼　宗務本部総裁室長代理　兼　総合本部アドバイザー　兼　政務本部活動推進参謀　兼　国際本部活動推進参謀）

立木秀学（理事　兼　HS 政経塾長）

※質問順。役職は収録当時のもの。

1 America's Founding Father Washington Appears

Masayuki Isono Now, we will start the spiritual interview with George Washington. Thank you very much, Master Ryuho Okawa.

Ryuho Okawa OK. Then, let's start. We are going to New York soon*, so the spiritual teaching of George Washington is very important, I think. This is the starting point of the United States of America and today, we have an opportunity to hear from him. So, we'd like to try. Then, is it OK?

We'd like to summon the spirit of the first president of the United States, George Washington. Mr. George Washington, the spirit of George Washington, would you come down here? We'd like to summon the spirit of George Washington, the first president of the

---

* On October 2nd, 2016, Master Okawa gave an English lecture titled, "Freedom, Justice, and Happiness" at Crowne Plaza Times Square Manhattan, New York.

1 「アメリカ建国の父」ワシントン登場

磯野将之 ただいまより、ジョージ・ワシントンの霊言を始めさせていただきます。大川隆法総裁先生、まことにありがとうございます。

大川隆法 はい。では、始めましょうか。私たちは近々、ニューヨークに行くことになっていますので（注）、ジョージ・ワシントンの霊示は非常に重要であると思います。これはアメリカ合衆国の原点です。今日はご本人から聞ける機会ですので、やってみたいと思います。よろしいですか。

　合衆国の初代大統領である、ジョージ・ワシントンの霊をお招きしたいと思います。ジョージ・ワシントン氏よ、ジョージ・ワシントンの霊よ、ここに降りたまえ。合衆国初代大統領、ジョージ・ワシントンの霊をお招きしたいと思います。

（注）2016年10月2日、アメリカ・ニューヨークのCrowne Plaza Times Square Manhattanにて、大川総裁は「Freedom, Justice, and Happiness」と題し英語説法を行った。

United States.

Isono Good morning.

George Washington Hmm…

Isono Are you…

Washington Good morning.

Isono …President George Washington?

Washington Yeah.

Isono Thank you very much for coming here today. It's a great honor to have you here. We will be more than happy to ask you several questions about yourself, the mission of America and its current situation. Is it OK?

1 「アメリカ建国の父」ワシントン登場

磯野　おはようございます。

ジョージ・ワシントン　うーん。

磯野　あなたは……。

ワシントン　おはよう。

磯野　ジョージ・ワシントン大統領でいらっしゃいますか。

ワシントン　いかにも。

磯野　本日は、お越しくださり、まことにありがとうございます。たいへん光栄です。あなたご自身について、またアメリカの使命や現在の状況について、質問させていただければ幸いです。よろしいでしょうか。

1 America's Founding Father Washington Appears

Washington OK, OK, OK.

Isono OK. Thank you very much. Firstly, I'd like to ask you about the mission of the United States because you are the founding president of the United States. The United States has been a great nation, a leading nation of the world for the past several decades. So, could you tell us what the mission of the United States of America is?

Washington Ahh…the United States is the new utopia of the world that was founded in the past 200 years. I had a special mission from God. "George Washington, please open a new world. This is the Land of Canaan* for you with the new immigrants from Europe. This nation will be the new leader of the world after the 18th or 19th century." So, this was a great mission.

---

* The land that God promised to give to the Israelites in the Old Testament. In the bible, it is described as "land flowing with milk and honey." Moses led the Israelites out of Egypt and headed to the Land of Canaan.

1 「アメリカ建国の父」ワシントン登場

ワシントン　オーケー、いいとも。

磯野　はい。ありがとうございます。まず初めに、あなたは合衆国を建国された大統領であられますので、合衆国の使命についてお伺いしたいと思います。合衆国は、ここ数十年間、世界をリードしている大国です。そこで、アメリカ合衆国の使命とは何か教えていただけますでしょうか。

ワシントン　ああ……。アメリカとは、ここ２００年で創設された、世界の新たなユートピアである。私は、神の特別の使命を担（にな）っていたんだ。「ジョージ・ワシントンよ、新たなる世界を開きたまえ。この地が、ヨーロッパからの移住者を迎えた、汝（なんじ）らの新たなるカナンの地（注）である。この国が、18世紀あるいは19世紀以降、世界の新たな導きとなるのだ」と。偉大な使命だった。神は、「汝は新た

（注）旧約聖書に出てくる、神がイスラエルの民に与えると約束した土地。聖書のなかでは「乳と蜜の流れる場所」と表現される。モーセはイスラエルの民を導いて出エジプトをなし、カナンの地を目指した。

1 America's Founding Father Washington Appears

God told me, "You are the new Adam, the new Moses," or something like that. This was my mission.

America is the greatest country in the world now. At the time of my presidency, it was a small country. The country's land was very huge but the country's power itself was very, very small. We became independent from the United Kingdom by the help of France. So at first, we were people who ran away from the United Kingdom and other countries, but nowadays, we are the champions of the world.

Isono OK.

なアダム、新たなモーセである」というふうに言われた。それが私の使命だった。

　今やアメリカは、世界の最大国である。私の大統領時代には小国だった。国土は広大だが、国力自体は非常に小さかった。フランスの支援を受けてイギリスから独立することができた。最初は、私たちはイギリスなどから逃げ延びてきた者たちだったが、今日(こんにち)では、われらこそ世界の王者なんだ。

磯野　分かりました。

2 In the American Presidential Election, He Supports the "Honest Man"

Yuta Okawa Thank you very much for coming to Happy Science today.

Washington Uh-huh.

Yuta Okawa My first question is simple. What is your hot issue now?

Washington Hot issue?

Yuta Okawa Yes, in Heaven.

Washington Heaven!?

Yuta Okawa Or from your viewpoint.

Washington Or Hell? [*Laughs.*]

2 米大統領選では、あの「正直者」を応援

大川裕太　本日は幸福の科学にお越しくださり、まことにありがとうございます。

ワシントン　ああ、はい。

大川裕太　私の最初の質問は、シンプルなものです。あなたが現在、注目されている問題は何でしょうか。

ワシントン　注目している問題かね。

大川裕太　はい。天上界で。

ワシントン　天上界で!?

大川裕太　もしくは、あなたの目からご覧になって。

ワシントン　もしくは、地獄でかな？（笑）

Yuta Okawa [*Laughs.*] I don't know. So…

Washington [*Laughs.*] I'm joking. Hot issue is, of course, the American presidency.

Yuta Okawa Uh-huh.

Washington The race for the presidency. Hot issue is how to knock down Hillary Clinton, of course [*laughs*].

Yuta Okawa [*Laughs.*] OK. So, I guess you're now supporting a candidate in the United States presidential election.

Washington Uh-huh.

Yuta Okawa What's his name?

Washington His name? It's the name for a *card* [*laughs*].

大川裕太　（笑）それは存じませんが……。

ワシントン　（笑）冗談だよ。注目している問題は、やはり、アメリカ大統領選だね。

大川裕太　ああ、はい。

ワシントン　大統領選の争いだよ。注目は、やはり、ヒラリー・クリントンをどう倒すかだな（笑）。

大川裕太　（笑）分かりました。では現在、あるアメリカ大統領候補者を支持されているわけですね。

ワシントン　そうだよ。

大川裕太　その方の名前は？

ワシントン　名前？　カードと同じ名前だね（笑）。

2 In the American Presidential Election, He Supports the "Honest Man"

[Interviewers laugh.]

Yuta Okawa OK.

Isono Maybe a trump card?

Washington Yeah, a *trump* card [*laughs*]*.

Yuta Okawa OK.

Washington The American joker, you know?

(質問者一同　笑)

大川裕太　なるほど。

磯野　トランプ・カード（切り札）でしょうか。

ワシントン　そう、トランプ・カード（笑・注）。

大川裕太　はい。

ワシントン　アメリカの「ジョーカー」だよ。お分かりかな。

（注）2016年1月4日、大川総裁はドナルド・トランプ氏の守護霊霊言を英語で収録。同霊言でトランプ守護霊は自身の過去世がジョージ・ワシントンであると発言している（『守護霊インタビュー　ドナルド・トランプ　アメリカ復活への戦略』参照）。
★ On January 4th, 2016, Master Okawa conducted a spiritual interview with Donald Trump's guardian spirit in English. His guardian spirit claims that Trump was George Washington in a previous life. (Refer to: *The Trump Card in the United States* [Tokyo: HS Press, 2016].)

Isono [*Laughs.*] Yes.

Yuta Okawa OK. I think the typical image of the first president, George Washington, was that he was very…

Washington Honest!

Yuta Okawa Honest, yeah.

Washington Reliable.

Yuta Okawa Reliable.

Washington Responsible.

Yuta Okawa But the American people depict you as a very serious and calm person. That's our image about you. But…

磯野　（笑）はい。

大川裕太　はい。初代ワシントン大統領の典型的なイメージは、非常に……。

ワシントン　正直！

大川裕太　正直、そうですね。

ワシントン　頼れる。

大川裕太　頼れる。

ワシントン　責任感が強い。

大川裕太　ただ、米国民は、非常に真面目で落ち着いた人物として、あなたを描いています。それが私たちのあなたのイメージなのですが……。

Washington Strong and what?

Yuta Okawa Strong, calm and…

Washington Cor?

Yuta Okawa *Calm.*

Washington Cold?

Yuta Okawa Calm.

Washington Colb?

Yuta Okawa Very quiet, you know? Your image…

Washington Ah, I know.

Yuta Okawa …in the movies, for example.

ワシントン　強くて、何ですか。

大川裕太　強くて落ち着いた（calm）……。

ワシントン　Cor？

大川裕太　「落ち着いた」です。

ワシントン　冷たい（Cold）？

大川裕太　「落ち着いた」。

ワシントン　Colb?

大川裕太　とても「静かな」人です。イメージですが……。

ワシントン　ああ、そうか。

大川裕太　例えば、映画に出てくるイメージです。

Washington Image? Ah…

Yuta Okawa Yeah, the typical image of you. But now, the real Mr. Donald Trump is a little different…

Washington OK, OK, OK, OK, OK.

Yuta Okawa …from your typical image, so….

Washington I got it.

Yuta Okawa We may misunderstand your personality.

Washington George Washington, the first president, was good at fighting, as you know. He was the commander-in-chief of the United States who fought against the United Kingdom. I am good at fighting.

Nowadays, we don't fight against our rivals with

ワシントン　イメージ？　ああ。

大川裕太　はい。あなたの典型的なイメージです。しかし、現実のドナルド・トランプ氏は少し違うかと……。

ワシントン　はい、はい、はい、はい、はい。

大川裕太　……あなたの典型的イメージからは。そこで……。

ワシントン　分かりました。

大川裕太　私たちは、あなたの個性に関して誤解しているのかもしれません。

ワシントン　初代大統領ジョージ・ワシントンは知っての通り、戦いに強かった。英国と戦った合衆国最高司令官だ。私は戦いが得意なんでね。

　現代ではライバルとの戦いに、剣や銃や矢なんかは使わ

a sword, gun, arrow or something like that. We fight against our competitors using only words, so words are the weapon nowadays. This is the reason I changed my strategy. That's the reason. We, who want to be a statesman like a president or a governor, must fight against our rivals and huge mass media using words, so words are very important these days. That is our new weapon.

Yuta Okawa Thank you. Yeah, we agree with that opinion. Mr. Donald Trump, himself, is very honest, too.

ない。言葉だけで相手と戦うので、現代では「言葉」が武器だ。だから私は戦略を変えたんだよ。それが理由だ。われわれ、大統領や知事などの政治家になろうとする者は、ライバルや巨大マスコミと言葉で戦わなければならない。だから、今は言葉が非常に重要になっている。これが新しい武器なんだ。

大川裕太　ありがとうございます。はい、私たちも同意見です。ドナルド・トランプ氏ご本人も、たいへん正直な方ですし。

ワシントンはアメリカ独立戦争（1775‒1783）を総司令官として戦い勝利に導いた。写真は「デラウェア川を渡るワシントン」（エマヌエル・ゴットリーブ・ロイツェ画、メトロポリタン美術館所蔵）。

Washington, as the commander-in-chief, led America to victory in the American War of Independence (1775~1783). Pictured is *Washington Crossing the Delaware* (Emanuel Gottlieb Leutze, Metropolitan Museum of Art).

Washington Honest! Yeah, it's a good word. Please print these words in Gothic and in big print. "**Honest man. Honest man, Donald Trump!**" Oh, yeah, it's good.

Yuta Okawa Other existing politicians in Washington D.C. use superficial words, but they are hiding something, I feel. So, Mr. Donald Trump is very…

Washington Honest! Yeah.

Yuta Okawa Yeah, honest.

Washington Yeah, honest! Hmm.

Yuta Okawa It's his personality, I think.

Washington It means I'm strong. Because of my strength, I can be honest. If politicians speak honestly,

ワシントン　正直！　そう、いい言葉だね。この言葉をゴシック体で大きく印刷してくれたまえ。**正直な男**。**正直者ドナルド・トランプ**。そう、いいねえ。

大川裕太　ワシントンDCにいる、現状のほかの政治家たちは、表向きは正しいことを言うのですが、何か隠していると思います。ですから、ドナルド・トランプさんは非常に……。

ワシントン　正直！　そうですよ。

大川裕太　はい。正直です。

ワシントン　そう、正直！　うん。

大川裕太　そこが彼の個性だと思います。

ワシントン　私が強いということだよ。強さゆえに、正直になれる。政治家が正直に話すと、マスメディアがその言

the mass media will attack them because of those words, so they want to hide their real thoughts. They use other words or hide their real political intentions.

So, these days, to be honest means to be strong. We are running through a field where bullets of mass media are flying from both sides, so it's very difficult. But I'm Captain America, so I can fight against them. My strength is my honesty.

Yuta Okawa Thank you very much.

3 On Racial Problems in Current America

Washington [*Sees Tsuiki attempting to ask a question.*] Ah, a silent man.

Shugaku Tsuiki Ah, thank you very much.

葉を取り上げて攻撃するものだから、政治家は本当に考えていることを隠したがる。別の言葉を使ったり、政治的な本心を隠したりする。

　だから現代では、「正直である」とは「強い」ということだ。右からも左からもマスメディアの銃弾が飛び交(か)っている中を走っているので、すごく大変なんだが、私は「キャプテン・アメリカ」だから彼らと戦える。私の強みは正直さだ。

大川裕太　ありがとうございます。

3　現代アメリカの人種問題について

ワシントン　（質問しようとしている立木に）ああ、物言わぬ男か。

立木秀学　はい、ありがとうございます。

Washington He will speak nothing.

Tsuiki Uh…

Washington [*Laughs.*]

Tsuiki Sorry, what I would like to ask you is about the ethnic problems. Now in the United States, one of the hot issues is the racial problem.

Washington Racial problem. OK.

Tsuiki One of the problems is the black people.

Washington Black people.

Tsuiki They are often shot by policemen*, and people get angry. What do you think about that?

---

* On September 20th, 2016, a black man was shot to death with a gun by a white police officer in Charlotte, North Carolina. This incident is controversial because there is a possibility that the man was not armed. Similar cases have occurred in recent years, causing widespread protests in America.

3 現代アメリカの人種問題について

ワシントン　この人は何も話さんよ。

立木　えー……。

ワシントン　ハッハッハッハッハ（笑）。

立木　すみません。お尋ねしたいのは、民族問題についてです。現在、アメリカで議論になっている問題の一つは、人種差別問題です。

ワシントン　人種差別か。オーケー。

立木　一つは黒人の問題です。

ワシントン　黒人か。

立木　黒人が警察官に撃たれることがよくあり（注）、人々は怒りを覚えています。それについてはどう思われますか。

（注）2016年9月20日、米ノースカロライナ州のシャーロットで黒人男性が白人警察官に銃で撃たれ死亡したが、男性は銃を所持していなかった可能性があり問題となっている。近年アメリカでは同種の事件が相次ぎ、抗議デモが広がっている。

3 On Racial Problems in Current America

Washington Uh-huh. OK, we have a lot of racial problems. One is, of course, the black problem. Another is the Hispanic problem and yet another is, of course, the Islamic problem. We have at least these three problems.

So firstly, there is the black problem, but we already have a black president. I forgot his name. Was it Black Obama or something like that?

Isono Yes, Obama.

Washington Ah, is that his name? We have a black president, President "Black Obama." So, it's a good news for black people that a black person became the president. At the least, they can be a president in the future, the next president or in the 21st or 22nd century. This means that they have political power nowadays, so it's good.

The next issue might be the presidency for ladies. This is a chance for ladies to become a president. It

3　現代アメリカの人種問題について

ワシントン　ああ、オーケー。人種問題はいろいろ抱えている。一つは、もちろん黒人問題。また、ヒスパニック問題と、やはりイスラム問題、少なくともこの三つの問題がある。

　まず黒人問題だが、すでに黒人大統領がいるのでね。名前を失念したが、「ブラック・オバマ」とか言ったかな。

磯野　はい、オバマです。

ワシントン　ああ、そんな名前だったかな。「ブラック・オバマ」という黒人大統領がいる。だから、黒人大統領が出たことは黒人にとっては福音だよ。少なくとも将来、次の大統領か、21世紀や22世紀には大統領になれるだろう。彼らに現在、政治的な力があるということだから、結構なことだね。

　次の問題は、女性大統領だろう。女性が大統領になれるチャンスだよ。それがヒラリー・クリントンの意味だが、

means Hillary Clinton. However, I don't think she is a real lady [*laughs*]. She was the First Lady to Bill Clinton, so it's not the problem of sexual discrimination.

If another lady who has made her way up by herself became a candidate for the presidency, I will appreciate it. But Hillary Clinton's capability is a little different. She benefits from Bill Clinton's halo, her husband. So we, the American people, dislike two presidents coming from one couple. I think it's against democracy. That's not democracy. That belongs to personal benefits. So, this is another problem. OK. Then, the next is, ah, did you only ask me about the black problem?

Tsuiki Ah, the black people, the Hispanic people and so on.

Washington I don't dislike Hispanic people. But in reality, please analyze the social situation of the United States. We have a lot of crimes in our country and the reason why is the immigrants from Mexico. They

彼女が本物のレディーだとは思えないね（笑）。ビル・クリントンのファースト・レディーだった人だから、性差別の問題じゃないんだよ。

　誰か別の、自分の力で上がってきた女性が大統領候補なら、評価するけどね。ヒラリー・クリントンの能力は少し違う。夫のビル・クリントンの七光（ななひかり）だから。われわれアメリカ人は、一組のカップルから大統領が二人出るなんて嫌（いや）だね。民主主義に反するだろう。民主主義じゃない。個人的な利点に属することだ。これがもう一つの問題だな。オーケー。それから次の、おっと、聞かれたのは黒人問題だけだったかな。

立木　はい、黒人やヒスパニックの人々などです。

ワシントン　ヒスパニックは嫌いじゃないよ。だが現実には、アメリカの社会問題を分析してもらいたいね。国内は犯罪で溢（あふ）れていて、理由はメキシコからの移民だよ。彼らは麻薬は運んでくるわ、犯罪を働く傾向があるわ、当然、

come with drugs, the tendency of criminality and of course, mafia-like business style.

So, I don't hate them but I just ask them before they become real Americans, "Please love America, the United States of America." It's the fundamental condition for them to be American. If they want to destroy our country, I will and we will resist against their tendencies.

Mexican people have envy toward the wealthy people in the United States. So, they want to intrude into the United States and become rich. To be rich is not a good thing in itself. We want to be rich for the purpose of a good aim, I mean to help other people, to help build God's state in this world or to help other countries who suffer from intrusions from a huge country. Something like that. So, I want them to have a frame of mind as a true American. This is the problem.

Some of the Mexican people are good people, of course, but others just seek to get money. That's a problem. They want to get money and it's easy to

マフィア的なビジネスのやり方も持ち込むからね。

　嫌いなわけではないが、ただ、彼らにはお願いしたい。本物のアメリカ人になる前に、「アメリカ合衆国を愛してください」と。彼らがアメリカ人になるためには、それが根本条件だ。わが国を駄目にしたいのなら、そんな傾向性には対抗せざるを得ない。

　メキシコ人は金持ちのアメリカ人がうらやましくて、アメリカに入り込んで金持ちになりたいんだよ。だが、金持ちになることそのものが、良いわけじゃない。われわれが豊かになりたいのは、善なる目的のためだ。つまり、人助けをするとか、この世界に神の国を創るお手伝いをするとか、大国に侵攻されて苦しんでいる国を助けるとか。ぜひ、本物のアメリカ人として、ふさわしい心を持ってほしいと思っている。問題はそこだな。

　もちろん、いいメキシコ人もいるが、金儲けしか考えていない奴もいる。問題はそこだ。金儲けがしたいから、ドラッグなどで儲けて金持ちになるのは簡単だが、その結果、

grow rich using drugs and things like that. But in the end, it will mean the ruin of a healthy society, so I hate them in this meaning. Of course, I know equality and I respect equality of the people as the members of the United States, but we must love our country. That's the reason. And oh…another one?

Yuta Okawa Islamic…

Washington Islamic, ah, it's difficult. It's a very difficult problem. Just now, we experienced an Islamic attack in New York*. It's troublesome for you too, because you are scheduled to hold a great lecture in New York. It's troublesome. He, meaning the criminal, is an American citizen, but he is an Islamic believer; he experienced being in a lot of Islamic countries and strengthened his faith. He did bad things against the U.S. citizens. If

---

★ On September 17th, 2016, blasts in the roads of Chelsea, New York left 29 injured. An American man from Afghanistan was placed in custody as a suspect.

健全な社会が滅んでしまう。その点があるから、私は彼らを好きになれないね。もちろん私も平等ということは知っているし、米国民としての平等は尊重しているが、自分の国は愛さなければ駄目だ。そういうわけです。それから、えーと……。

大川裕太　イスラム教徒……。

ワシントン　イスラム教徒ね、これは難しい。実に難しい問題だ。この前もニューヨークでイスラム教徒による攻撃があったけど（注）、君たちにとっても困った問題だろう。ニューヨークで大講演会をやる予定だから、困ったものだね。犯人は米国民だがイスラム教徒で、いろんなイスラム教国での経験を経てイスラム信仰を強め、米国民に被害を与えた。そんなことがしたかったら、イスラム国かアフガニスタンか、どこかに帰れというんだ。アメリカ人でいる

（注）2016年9月17日、米ニューヨーク・チェルシー地区の大通りで大きな爆発が起き29人が負傷。アフガニスタン出身のアメリカ人男性が容疑者として身柄を拘束された。

he wants to do so, he must go back to IS, Afghanistan or another country. He should not be an American citizen. That's what I think.

4 He Helped God Make a New Civilization

Yuta Okawa Historically, it was recorded that you hated Native Americans.

Washington Hahaha.

Yuta Okawa Your words remain, "They, American Indians, are beasts of prey." However, it was also recorded that you were very kind to your own black slaves in your home. So, I think Mr. Trump's tendency is very similar to your opinion on racial problems. What was your thought on races?

べきじゃないと思うね。

4　神が新文明を拓くのを手伝った

大川裕太　歴史の記録によれば、あなたはアメリカ先住民が嫌いだったということです。

ワシントン　ははは。

大川裕太　「彼ら、つまり先住民は、猛獣だ」という、あなたの言葉も残っています。しかし、家では、黒人奴隷に対して非常に優しかったという記録もあります。ですから、トランプ氏の傾向性は、人種問題についてのあなたのご意見と良く似ていると思うのですが、人種に関しては、どういったお考えだったのでしょうか。

4　He Helped God Make a New Civilization

Washington Of course, this land of North America historically belonged to the Native Americans. But this land is very huge and affluent. It was a new Canaan, flowing with milk and honey. It was a new land of hope. We thought God would be pleased by the prosperity brought through advanced people. So, we came from Europe as the Pilgrim Fathers* or in another name, Puritans.

We aimed at setting up a new country of God in this area. So, this was a heavenly battle between the god of Native American Indians and the god of Pilgrim Fathers. European gods wanted to be separated from their old-fashioned worship and wanted to set up a new religion and a new social movement, which in the political meaning, was an experiment of democratic politics in this world.

Of course, the Native American Indians had their

---

* Puritans who traveled from England to America on a ship called Mayflower in hopes for religious freedom in 1620.

4　神が新文明を拓くのを手伝った

ワシントン　もちろん、この北アメリカという土地は、歴史的には先住民のものだった。しかし、この土地は、すごく広大で豊かだからね。要するに、乳と蜜の流れる新たな「カナンの地」だったんだよ。新たな希望の地だ。神は、進んでいる人々が繁栄をもたらすことを喜ばれるだろうということで、われわれは「ピルグリム・ファーザーズ」(注)としてヨーロッパから渡ってきた。またの名を「清教徒(ピューリタン)」とも言った。

　われわれはこの地に、新たな神の国を建国しようとした。だから、あの世で先住民の神とピルグリム・ファーザーズの神が戦ったわけだ。ヨーロッパの神々が、彼らの古い信仰から切り離して新しい宗教を立ち上げ、新たな社会運動というか、政治的に言えば民主主義政治という文明実験をこの世で始めようと思ったわけです。

　当然、先住民には財産も権利もあったが、神は、われわ

(注) 1620年、信仰の自由を求めてメイフラワー号でアメリカに渡ったイギリスの清教徒(ピューリタン)のこと。

properties and rights, but God hoped that we would become the new masters. So, we did our best. Our mission was to open the frontier for the future, a new frontier.

We succeeded in our plans. We got rich and we showed our gods the prosperity of the New America. In another name, this was called the New Atlantis. Therefore, this is a matter of civilization. If the original God wants to make a new civilization, it's good to help Him. That's the reason.

Yes, I hired 40 or at most, almost 100 black slaves. But at that time, this was allowed. So I, myself, was a successful planter and became a rich man. It's my typical feature to be a rich man. I was rich and also a good commander-in-chief who was good at fighting against enemies.

And in addition to that, I was a statesman or politician—in a good meaning. I can be called the first politician of the United States. It meant I could separate enemies from our friends, and after that, settle

れが新たな主人になることを望まれた。だから、われわれは力を尽くした。未来のフロンティア、新たなフロンティアを切り拓く使命があったんだよ。

　その計画は成功した。われわれは豊かさを実現し、神々に新たなアメリカの繁栄を示すことができた。それが別名、「ニュー・アトランティス」とも呼ばれた。だから、文明の問題なんだ。根源の神が新文明を築こうとされているなら、そのお手伝いをするのは「善なる行為」である。そういう理由だよ。

　確かに、私は40人か、多い時は100人近い黒人奴隷を使っていたけれども、当時は認められていたことだからね。だから私自身、大農場主で、大金持ちになった。大金持ちであるというのが、私の典型的な特徴なんです。大金持ちで、かつ、敵とよく戦うことのできる優秀な最高司令官だった。

　なおその上、いい意味での政治家でもあった。アメリカの最初の政治家だったと言ってもいい。要するに、敵と味方を区別したことはしたけれども、敵味方の間の問題を解決することができたし、支配層と被支配層の間の問題も解

the problem between them. Also, I could settle the problem between dominant people and people who were under their control. This is the starting point of a politician or statesman. So, I had three functions: commander-in-chief, a rich planter and politician. This was a blessing for the new America. Haha!

Isono Thank you.

5 On America's Foreign Policies on the Middle East and Russia

Tsuiki I would like to ask a question about diplomacy.

Washington Diplomacy? OK.

Tsuiki How do you think the United States should cope with the Islamic State?

決することができた。これは、政治家の原点にあたる部分だからね。であるからして、私は「司令官」と「大農場主」と「政治家」という三つの機能を担っていたわけだ。これこそ新興国アメリカにとって、「神の恵み」というものだったね。ハハ！

磯野　ありがとうございます。

5　米国の中東・ロシア外交について

立木　外交についてご質問したいと思います。

ワシントン　外交かね。いいよ。

立木　アメリカはイスラム国に、どう対処すべきであると思われますか。

5 On America's Foreign Policies on the Middle East and Russia

Washington Hmm, ah, it's a little complicated. Firstly, I will support the country of Israel. They already have 200 nuclear missiles as former Secretary of State Powell spilled the beans*. On the other hand, Islamic countries don't have nuclear weapons nowadays. So, although there is a great difference between the population of Islamic countries and that of Israel, this power of nuclear bomb brings a balance of power. Therefore, we will support Israeli nuclear armament and we want to suppress the Islamic states. This is the first point.

Another point is Vladimir Putin. He has some kind of ambition to get Syria and control other Islamic states. We must cooperate with Mr. Putin. You must talk with him to make sure that the oil problem doesn't cause the next great war. Russia is in an economic crisis now, so they need new customers for their market. I must

---

* On September 16th, 2016, it was reported that Colin Powell, a former secretary of state, sent a private email to an acquaintance mentioning that Israel held 200 nuclear weapons in March of 2015. In fact, Israel is considered to be a state with nuclear weapons, but has not formally admitted it.

5　米国の中東・ロシア外交について

ワシントン　うーん。ああ、それは少しばかり面倒な問題だね。まず、私はイスラエルを支持する。パウエル元国務長官が漏らした通り（注）、イスラエルはすでに核ミサイルを200発、保有している。だが一方のイスラム諸国は、現段階では核兵器を保有していない。だから、イスラム諸国とイスラエルの人口の差は大きいけれども、この核爆弾の力が両者の「力の均衡(きんこう)」をもたらしている。だから、われわれはイスラエルの核武装を支持し、イスラム諸国を押さえ込んでおきたいと考えている。これが第一点だね。

　もう一点は、ウラジーミル・プーチンだ。プーチンは、シリアを手に入れて他のイスラム諸国も支配下に置きたいという野心めいたものを抱いている。プーチン氏とは協力しなければならない。石油問題が次の大戦につながることがないように、彼と話す必要がある。ロシアは今、経済危機だから、ロシア市場にとっての新たな顧客を必要として

（注）2016年9月16日、コリン・パウエル元米国務長官が、2015年3月に「イスラエルは200発の核兵器を保有している」と知人宛の私用メールで言及していたと報じられた。イスラエルは事実上、核保有国とされているが、公式には認めていない。

rebalance the power between Russia and America.

You already know that I love the isolation of America, but this is a misunderstanding. I don't just say isolation, I want to make new power in the United States *and* rebalance the world. After that, I want the United States to be the dominant country again and take new leadership. I will realize these desires in the next eight years.

6 On American and World Economies

Yuta Okawa Thank you. Next, I'd like to ask about the American and world economies.

Washington OK.

Yuta Okawa President George Washington, your first career was a land surveyor. You made your living by

いる。私は、ロシアとアメリカのパワーバランスを再調整しないといけない。

　私が孤立したがっているということは先刻ご承知だろうけど、それは誤解です。単に孤立を言ってるわけじゃなくて、アメリカの国力を新たに立て直し、その上で、世界のバランスを取り戻し、それから最強国に返り咲いて、アメリカが新たにリーダーシップを取ろうと思っているわけでね。次の８年で実現してみせるさ。

6　アメリカ経済と世界経済について

大川裕太　ありがとうございます。次に、アメリカ経済と世界経済について伺いたいと思います。

ワシントン　どうぞ。

大川裕太　あなたは、ジョージ・ワシントン大統領は、最初の経歴としては土地の測量士をされていました。測量で

that and you got rich. Now, Mr. Donald Trump is also very rich through trading real estates. His and your vocations are very similar, I guess.

Washington Yeah.

Yuta Okawa I think you are one of the specialists on economy. So, how can you revive the American economy and its position in the world economy?

Washington Hmm...OK, OK. In my days, America was a small country in its activities and its power, in the economic meaning, of course. Now, it's number one in the world, although, it's declining a little.

The first problem is how to compete with the Chinese economy. Next one will be Japan, India or Germany. So, firstly, I'm thinking about the Chinese economy. They are doing too much. I don't want to say anything if they are acting within their own ability or capability, or within their real economic power.

生計を立てて富を築かれましたが、現在、ドナルド・トランプ氏もまた不動産業で大きな富を築きましたので、お二人の職業は非常に似ていると思います。

ワシントン　そうです。

大川裕太　経済の専門家でいらっしゃると思いますので。どうすれば、アメリカ経済と、世界経済におけるその地位を復活させることができるでしょうか。

ワシントン　うーん、はい、分かった。私の時代は、アメリカの活動は小規模だったし、経済力も小さかったけど、現在は世界のナンバーワンだ。少し傾きかけてはいるけどね。

　最初の問題は、中国経済とどう競争していくかだ。その次が、日本やインドやドイツ。だから、まずは中国経済のことを考えてる。中国は、やり過ぎだね。自分たちの能力や器の範囲で、実体経済の力の範囲内でやってる分には、何も言うつもりはないし、構わんけれど、高望みし過ぎだよ。中国は覇権国になろうとして、政治面でも経済面でも

That's OK. But they have too much ambition. They want to become a hegemonic country and control the Asian and African countries in the political and economic meanings. They are even tempted to control the European countries. This is the great problem.

In addition to that, they have, for example, the South Asian islands problem, the Spratly Islands problem. The real problem is that they are approaching Russia; both China and Russia are cooperating in conducting joint exercises. They are cooperating to go against the United States.

So, I want to divide the two powers, China and Russia. I now want to make a new friendship with Vladimir Putin. Mr. Putin and I can be friends, I think, because he has great leadership. He is more skilled in controlling his political power than Mr. Obama. So, if I can become the next president—ah, not *can become*, I *will be* the next president—we, Putin and Donald Trump, or George Washington, will be good friends because we have respect for each other. We can

アジアやアフリカの国々を支配しようとしている。さらにはヨーロッパまで支配下に置きたい気になってるんで、大問題だ。

　その上さらに、例えば南アジアの島々にも南沙諸島の問題がある。本当の問題は、中国がロシアに近づこうとして、中国とロシアが共同軍事演習をやってることだ。アメリカに対抗するために協力しているわけだ。

　だから私は、中国とロシア、二つの強国を引き離したいんだよ。今はウラジーミル・プーチンと新たに友好関係を結びたいと思ってる。プーチン氏とは友達になれると思う。強いリーダーシップがある人だからね。オバマさんより、政治力を操る手腕があるから。私が次期大統領になれたら、ああ、「なれたら」じゃなくて、次期大統領に「なる」わけだから、プーチンとドナルド・トランプは──ジョージ・ワシントンかな？──良き友人になるよ。お互い、尊敬し合ってるし、互いの政治力や能力を評価できるからね。だ

estimate the political power or the capability of each other. So, we will cooperate with Russia.

Mr. Obama made a lot of mistakes. One of them is that he wanted to be an enemy of Russia because of the Crimean problem. I think Russia has the necessity to protect Crimean people because 65% of the Crimean people come from Russia. It's their duty. The EU also made a mistake. Thus, I support this point that Putin is not bad.

Another great mistake of Obama is that he is weak in the mind, so he wanted to decrease the power of nuclear weapons and tried to declare that the United States will never use nuclear weapons in its first attack. Now, the situation is unsettled because of the critiques from his colleagues. And South Korea and Japan are very afraid of North Korea, of course, so he must reconsider that.

I have the idea of controlling our war budget, but it doesn't mean that I want to destroy and weaken the American political power and the power of the U.S.

から、ロシアとは協力するよ。

　オバマさんは間違ってばかりだったから。その一つは、クリミア問題が理由でロシアの敵になろうとしたことだ。クリミアの住民の６５％はロシア出身なんだから、ロシアはクリミアを護る必要があるし、それが義務だろう。ＥＵも失敗したね。この点においては、プーチンは悪くないと支持したい。

　オバマがもう一つ、やらかした大間違いは、気が弱いので、核兵器の力を減らそうとして、「アメリカは絶対に、核による先制攻撃はしない」と宣言しようとしたことだ。今は同僚から批判されて、結論が出ていない状況だけど。当然、韓国と日本が北朝鮮を非常に恐れているので、その点は考え直さないと駄目だろう。

　私は、戦争関連予算は抑制したいという考えだ。ただし、アメリカの政治力を弱めて軍事力を衰退させたいわけじゃない。建設的な道を選びたいから、効果的なことにだけ集

army. I want to take a constructive way. I only want to focus on the effective matter. Before that, I or we need a conclusion, a decision against the new problem between two or three countries. I can make decisions, so it will be economical in the real meaning. I can use weapons in the context of the word, *economize*. This is not the weakness of the United States. This is efficient in managing our troops. We will, of course, ask our fellow countries, "If you want our cooperation, you have to pay your fair share." We will ask them. It's to strengthen America again.

7 On Problems with North Korea

Isono OK. Thank you. I'd like to ask your thoughts on North Korean problems.

Washington North Korean problems, OK.

中したいからだ。その前に、この二カ国あるいは三カ国間の新たな問題について判断を下さないといけない。私には判断できるから。これが本当の「経済性」だよ。「economize（経済化する＝節約する）」という言葉の文字通りの意味で、兵器を使用することができる。アメリカを弱体化させるわけじゃなく、軍の運用における効率性のためだ。そして、やはり同盟国に対しては、「私たちに協力してほしいのなら、費用面で応分の負担をしてほしい」とお願いしたいと思う。アメリカをもう一度強い国にするためにね。

7　北朝鮮問題について

磯野　はい、ありがとうございます。北朝鮮問題についてもお考えを伺いたいと思います。

ワシントン　北朝鮮問題、はい。

7 On Problems with North Korea

Isono This year, North Korea has conducted several missile launch tests and nuclear tests.

Washington Uh-huh.

Isono Now, the United Nations General Assembly is being held and the leaders of the world are discussing this issue. But I don't think they have a clear solution to this problem. So, I'd like to ask your thoughts on it.

Washington Ah, OK, OK, OK. The North Korean problem itself is not so difficult. It's a small country. We can defeat them within one month, so it's not so difficult.

The difficult problem is China. China is supporting North Korea, in reality. So, we must ask them, "Which do you like better? North Korea or the free trade with Western countries?" We will or I will insist about this issue. I want to separate the combination between these two countries.

磯野 今年、北朝鮮は複数回、ミサイル発射試験を実施しています。核実験も行っています。

ワシントン うん。

磯野 現在、国連総会が開かれており、世界の指導者がこの問題について議論していますが、明確な解決策はないように思います。どうお考えでしょうか。

ワシントン ああ、はい、はい、分かった。北朝鮮問題それ自体は、大して難しくない。小国だから、一カ月で倒せるんで、別に難しいことはない。

難しいのは中国問題のほうだ。実際には中国が北朝鮮を支援しているので、中国には、「北朝鮮と、西側との自由貿易と、どちらがいいか」と聞かないといけない。この点は主張していくつもりだよ。この二国間の連携を分断しないといけない。

China wants to use North Korea as a tool or the right hand or left hand of the Chinese army when a new war occurs between them and the United States, Japan or South Korea. That's the reason China or Beijing spoke that it's not good to set the THAAD missiles* in the bases of South Korea because these can protect against the missiles of China. This means they are thinking about the North Korean army as their tools to protect China from other countries. So firstly, I must separate these two countries in the political context.

Next is how to separate the combination between China and Russia. I will assist Russia and Russia can survive after that. Putin can survive. Japan can also be friends with Russia. If America and Japan can both be friends with Russia, Russia will choose this direction and keep some distance from China. After that, I will attack North Korea. There needs to be separation from

---

* Terminal High Altitude Area Defense missile. An interception system to shoot down an enemy's ballistic missile in its terminal phase. South Korea and America made a joint announcement on July 8th, 2016 that they agreed to deploy an American THAAD missile in South Korea.

中国は、アメリカや日本や韓国との間に戦争が始まったら、北朝鮮を道具として、言わば中国軍の右腕か左腕として使いたいわけだ。だからこそ中国政府は、「韓国の基地にＴＨＡＡＤ（サード）ミサイル（注）を配備するのはよくない」と主張している。中国のミサイルから防衛できてしまうからね。中国は北朝鮮軍を、他国から中国を守るための道具として使おうと思ってるということだよ。だから、まず、この二カ国を政治的に分断する必要がある。

その次が、中国とロシアの結びつきをどう分断するかだ。私はロシアを支援するから、ロシアはそれで生き延びる。プーチンは生き延びることができる。日本もロシアと友好関係を結べる。アメリカと日本が両方ともロシアと友好関係を結べるというなら、ロシアはその方向を選択して、中国とは距離を取るだろう。そうなった時が、私が北朝鮮を攻撃する時だ。北朝鮮を大国と分断することが必要で、北

（注）終末高高度防衛ミサイル（Terminal High Altitude Area Defense missile）。敵弾道ミサイルを終末段階で撃ち落とすための迎撃システム。米国と韓国は2016年7月8日、韓国に米国のＴＨＡＡＤミサイルを配備することで合意したと共同声明で発表した。

other greater countries. North Korea can be conquered in one month if alone. I think so. In the diplomatic meaning, I need good relationships with South Korea and Japan.

Another direction is to ask South Korea and Japan to protect themselves by nuclear weapons. North Korea is your potential enemy. So, it's your enemy, not the enemy of the United States of America. We are far from North Korea. They cannot fight against the United States. They can only attack the American base camps in places like Japan and South Korea. We will never be defeated by them.

I will, after great consideration, eventually ask South Korea and Japan to protect themselves by themselves. It's possible. If the U.S. insists that they protect themselves, this can become the world trend.

So, now is the time for Japan to change. Only the Happiness Realization Party's policy and Mr. Abe's hidden desire is to protect Japan by a stronger army. So, I will assist in that opinion. Japan is filled with left-

朝鮮一国だけなら一カ月で制圧できると思う。外交的には、韓国や日本との友好関係が必要だね。

　もう一つの方向性は、韓国と日本に「核兵器で自国を防衛してください」と頼むことだ。北朝鮮が潜在的な敵であるのは、君たちに対してだ。君たちの敵であって、米国の敵ではない。われわれは北朝鮮から遠いからね。アメリカと戦えるわけがない。せいぜい、日本や韓国などにある米軍基地を攻撃できるくらいで、アメリカが彼らに負けることはあり得ない。

　私は熟考を重ねたうえで、いずれは韓国と日本に、自分たちで国を護るよう頼むつもりだよ。可能なことだから。アメリカが君たちに向けて、「自分の力で国を護るべきだ」と主張すれば、それが世界のトレンドになることはあり得る。
　日本は今こそ、変わるべき時なんだ。軍を強くして日本を護ろうとしてるのは、幸福実現党の政策と、安倍さんが腹の中でそうしたいと思ってるだけだからさ。私がその意見を援護してやるよ。日本はマスメディアが左翼的言論一

wing opinions of the mass media. It's very difficult for politicians to make progress in defense, so I will assist. This is your future.

8 The Secret of the God of America

Yuta Okawa Thank you. I guess you are the highest spirit in the United States, *in Heaven*.

Washington Uh-huh. [*Laughs.*] OK.

Yuta Okawa [*Laughs.*] So, I think you know God's Will about the United States and God's plan for the United States in the next several decades. Could you tell us God's next plan for the United States and this world?

Washington It's your strong point. You are majoring in the hegemonic problem of countries. Oh, please

色で、政治家が国防を推し進めるのはきわめて難しいから、力を貸そうじゃないか。これが君たちの未来だな。

8 「アメリカの神」の秘密

大川裕太　ありがとうございます。あなたは、アメリカの最高指導霊でいらっしゃると思います。「天上界」で。

ワシントン　うん。(笑)オーケー。

大川裕太　(笑)ですから、アメリカについての神のご意志や、今後数十年のアメリカに関する神の計画を、ご存じだと思います。アメリカや世界に関する「次なる神の計画」をお教えいただけますでしょうか。

ワシントン　それこそ、君の強みじゃないか。各国の覇権の問題が専攻なんだろう。いや、ぜひ、アメリカが覇権を

teach me how to realize hegemony for America.

Yuta Okawa I think America is now having a hegemonic power, and thus, your strength will solve everything. I believe that if you were stronger than Xi Jinping and Vladimir Putin, you will realize hegemony.

Washington Hmm, OK. That's a good point. If, IF, *if*, Ms. Hillary Clinton becomes the next president, America will lose its hegemonic power over the world. I strongly insist on this point. So, the clever American people, without mistake, will choose me as the next president. It will bring new hope for America in the 21st, 22nd and the following centuries, I think. My success will make the next 300 years of prosperity in the United States.

Yuta Okawa One more question. Do you have specific friends in Heaven, spirits who are either American or other nationalities?

握るための方法を教えてくださいよ。

大川裕太　アメリカは今、覇権を手にしていると思いますし、それゆえ、あなたの強さが、すべてを解決すると思います。あなたが習近平やウラジーミル・プーチン以上に強ければ、覇権を握ることができると思います。

ワシントン　ああ、オーケー。それは大切なポイントだね。もし、仮に、「万が一」、ヒラリー・クリントン氏が次期大統領になったら、アメリカは世界の覇権を失う。この点は強く主張しておきたい。だから、賢明な米国民は、間違いなく私を次期大統領に選ぶだろう。それが21世紀、22世紀、それ以降の世紀における、アメリカの新たな希望となるだろう。私が成功することで、今後３００年続く、アメリカの「新たな繁栄」が拓かれるだろう。

大川裕太　もうひとつ質問があります。天上界のアメリカの霊人や、他の国の霊人で、特定の友人はいらっしゃいますか。

Washington I am the king of the United States, so no one can compare with me. Even the famous Lincoln just remade the United States. He was not the founder. He was a re-maker. So, I am in a higher position than Lincoln.

Isono Are you the top of the American spiritual world?

Washington No, there is the Creator.

Yuta Okawa Creator?

Washington So, I'm second to the Creator.

Isono If possible, could you please tell us the name of the Creator?

ワシントン　私はアメリカの〝国王〟なんだから、私と肩を並べる者はいないさ。かの有名なリンカンであっても、アメリカを再建しただけだからね。創始者じゃなくて、再建者だから。私のほうがリンカンより立場が上ですよ。

磯野　アメリカ霊界のトップでいらっしゃるということですか。

ワシントン　いや、創造主がいらっしゃる。

大川裕太　創造主ですか。

ワシントン　だから、私は創造主に次ぐ存在だな。

磯野　可能であれば、その創造主の名前を教えていただけますでしょうか。

Washington He says, "I'm Thoth*."

Isono Thoth?

Washington God Thoth.

Yuta Okawa OK. You were a disciple of Thoth?

Washington He said that he was the God of the Atlantic civilization†. He said that America is a newborn Atlantic civilization. He has such kind of mission to rebuild the Atlantic civilization again. So, he might be the God of America.

---

* A great spiritual leader who built the golden age of the Atlantic civilization around 12,000 years ago. He was known as the god of wisdom in ancient Egypt, and is also the branch spirit of the God of the Earth, El Cantare.

† A civilization that prospered on Atlantis in the Atlantic Ocean. Twelve thousand years ago, the Omniscient and Omnipotent Lord Thoth led Atlantis to the golden age, but the continent sank underwater 10,400 years ago. Refer to *The Laws of the Sun* (Ryuho Okawa, [Tokyo: HS Press, 2013]).

ワシントン 「われはトス（注１）なり」とおっしゃっている。

磯野 トスですか。

ワシントン トス神(しん)だよ。

大川裕太 分かりました。トス神の弟子でいらっしゃったのですか。

ワシントン ご自分のことを、アトランティス文明（注２）の神であると言われ、アメリカはアトランティス文明の新生した姿であると言われていた。アトランティス文明を再興する使命をお持ちだから、アメリカの神であるということかもしれないね。

（注１）約１万２千年前にアトランティス文明の最盛期を築いた大導師。古代エジプトでは智慧の神として知られていた。地球神エル・カンターレの分身。

（注２）大西洋上のアトランティス大陸に栄えた文明。１万２千年前に全知全能の主トスという大導師、大指導者を得て最盛期を迎えたが、１万４百年前、海中に没した。『太陽の法』（幸福の科学出版刊）参照。

Yuta Okawa Thank you very much.

Isono So, may I ask what is the name of God you believed in while you were alive? Was it God Thoth?

Washington Hmm?

Isono Oh, I mean…

Washington Ah, no, no, no, no. When I was living in the flesh, I was a Christian and of course believed in Jesus Christ. Through Jesus Christ, I believed in his Father. But I didn't know the name of our Father. Now, I know Him.

Isono OK. Historically, you were not only a Christian but also a member of Freemasonry*.

---

* A secret society, with approximately 6 million members around the world, that has been said to have prospered from a stonemason guild in Medieval Europe. They claim to be "a fraternal organization that seeks the self-improvement of its members and, through them, the improvement of society," but the details of their activities are not disclosed. Washington joined the Free Mason of Virginia in 1752.

8 「アメリカの神」の秘密

大川裕太　ありがとうございます。

磯野　生前に信じていらした神の名についてお聞きしてよろしいでしょうか。それはトス神だったのですか。

ワシントン　うん？

磯野　つまり……。

ワシントン　ああ、いや、いや、そうじゃない。肉体に宿っていた時はクリスチャンだったから、当然イエス・キリストを信じていたし、イエス・キリストを通して「天の父」を信じていたけど、「父」の名は知らなかった。今は知ってるけど。

磯野　分かりました。歴史によれば、あなたはクリスチャンでしたが、フリーメイソン（注）のメンバーでもありました。

（注）全世界に会員約600万人をもつ秘密結社で、中世ヨーロッパの石工職人のギルドから発展したと言われる。「会員相互の特性と人格の向上をはかり、良き人々をさらに良くしようとする団体」とされているが、具体的な活動内容は非公開。ワシントンは1752年、バージニアでフリーメイソンに加わった。

Washington Uh-huh. OK.

Isono So, could you tell us about your relation with Freemasonry?

Washington In reality, when I was a human, I didn't know clearly about the relationship between God and being a Freemason. But now, I understand that the real Grand Master of Freemasonry is God Hermes. So, I've been told God Hermes and God Thoth are the same consciousness. I've heard that the Thoth-Hermes-sovereignty* has taken leadership in these several thousand years, especially in the Western countries. So, the belief in Thoth and the belief in Hermes are not different, it's the same. I think so.

---

* In Ancient Egypt, there was the idea that the god of wisdom Thoth and Greek God Hermes were one entity. The concept that the entity guided Ancient Egypt was called the Thoth-Hermes-sovereignty and the entity of the two united was called "Hermes Trismegistus" (triple great Hermes). At Happy Science, it is revealed that God Thoth is the God of the Atlantic Civilization, that Hermes is the reincarnation of Thoth and that both are branch spirits of God of the Earth, El Cantare. Refer to *The Mystical Laws* (Ryuho Okawa, [Tokyo: HS Press, 2015]).

ワシントン　ああ、そうだ。

磯野　フリーメイソンとのご関係について教えていただけますでしょうか。

ワシントン　人間として生きていたときは、正直、「神」と「フリーメイソンであること」の関係性は、よく分からなかったんだが、今は、フリーメイソンの真のグランドマスター（大導師）はヘルメス神であると知っている。ヘルメス神とトス神は同じ意識体だと教わっている。ここ数千年は、特に西洋においては、トス神とヘルメス神の統治（トート＝ヘルメス体制・注）による指導がなされていたと聞いている。だから、「トス信仰」と「ヘルメス信仰」の二つは別々のものではなく、同じものだと思うね。

（注）古代エジプトには、エジプトの智慧の神であるトート神とギリシャのヘルメス神は一体であるとの思想があり、両者によるエジプト文明の指導体制は「トート＝ヘルメス体制」と言われ、両者が合体した存在は「ヘルメス・トリスメギストス（三倍偉大なヘルメス）」と呼ばれる。幸福の科学は、トート神とはアトランティス文明のトス神であり、トスもその転生であるヘルメスも地球神エル・カンターレの分身であることを明かしている。『神秘の法』（幸福の科学出版刊）参照。

9 His Past Lives as a God in India, Europe, and Africa

Yuta Okawa Thank you very much. The time is nearly up, so if you have any message toward the American people, could you please tell us?

Washington Oh, OK. My message is that I'm in the position of *Ame-no-Minakanushi** in Japan. You know, the central god of the universe. It's a good name, a big name, but I am the Ame-no-Minakanushi of Japan who was born in America. Not himself, but almost in equal position as his. So, we're friends.

Yuta Okawa OK, thank you very much. Yes, you are also very positive and honest.

---

* One of the central gods of Japanese Shintoism. Described in folk stories in the *Kojiki* (*Records of Ancient Matters*) as the original God. Happy Science has conducted spiritual research in the past and revealed that Yuta Okawa is the reincarnation of Ame-no-Minakanushi.

9 過去世はインド、ヨーロッパ、アフリカの神

大川裕太　ありがとうございます。お時間も近づいてきたようです。アメリカ国民に何かメッセージがございましたら、いただけますでしょうか。

ワシントン　ああ、はい。メッセージは、私は日本の天御中主神（注）と同じ立場にあるということです。あの「宇宙の中心神」です。素晴らしい名前ですが、私が「アメリカに生まれた日本の天御中主神」です。彼本人ではないが、ほぼ同じ立場です。だから君とは友だちなんだよ。

大川裕太　分かりました。どうもありがとうございます。はい、あなたも非常に積極的で正直な方ですよね。

（注）日本神道の中心的な神の一柱。古事記神話では根本神とされる。質問者の大川裕太は天御中主神の転生であることが以前の霊査で明らかになっている。

Washington Positive, yeah, of course. I'm positive, I have originality and I like creation. Yeah, that's the reason.

Yuta Okawa I feel an affinity between us. Thank you very much.

Isono If I may ask, could you tell us about your reincarnations or past lives?

Washington Past lives?

Isono Yes, before you were born as George Washington. Who were you?

Washington Ah...it's very difficult to say because I'm the original god of the United States of America. If I say I was born in another country, the American people will be very sad about that. So, it's very difficult, but if I can say a little, I was one of the gods of India, one

9　過去世はインド、ヨーロッパ、アフリカの神

ワシントン　それはもう積極的だよ。積極的で、独創性があって、創造することが好きだね。そういうわけだよ。

大川裕太　あなたには親しみを覚えます。どうもありがとうございます。

磯野　もしよろしければ、あなたの転生、つまり過去世について教えていただけないでしょうか。

ワシントン　過去世？

磯野　はい。ジョージ・ワシントンとして生まれる前は、どなただったのでしょうか。

ワシントン　ああ……アメリカの始原の神としては、非常に言いにくいな。違う国に生まれていたとしたら、アメリカ人はすごく残念がるから。だから言いにくいけど、少しだけ言えるとしたら、私はインドの神々の一人であり、ヨーロッパの神々の一人であり、アフリカの神々の一人でも

of the gods of Europe and one of the gods of Africa. I can say that.

Yuta Okawa Indian god? We know a lot of names of Indian gods. God Shiva*? Am I right?

Washington Ah, Shiva. Umm…is it a good meaning or not? Not Shiva, but the role is a little similar to Shiva.

Yuta Okawa Indra†?

Washington Indra? Hmm. Indra, Indra…I have another name, but how should I say…It's OK. It's about India, but I'm American, so don't worry.

★ One of the highest gods of Hinduism. God that controls destruction.

† A god of Hinduism. The Sakra devanam Indra of Buddhism.

あった。それくらいなら言える。

大川裕太　インドの神ですか。インドの神々の名前はいろいろありますが、シヴァ神（注１）ですか。

ワシントン　ああ、シヴァねえ。うーん……それはいい意味なのかな。シヴァではないが、役割としては、ややシヴァと似てるかな。

大川裕太　インドラ（注２）ですか。

ワシントン　インドラ？　うーん、インドラ、インドラ……。違う名前だけど、どう言えばいいかな……まあ、いいじゃないか。インドの話だし。私はアメリカ人だから、気にしなくていいよ。

（注１）ヒンドゥー教の最高神の一柱で、破壊をつかさどる神。
（注２）ヒンドゥー教の神。仏教でいう帝釈天のこと。

Isono Then, let's keep it a secret of yours.

Washington Anyway, I was the founder of a country or civilization, or a big name in the period of prosperity of a civilization. I was in the same situation as Ame-no-Minakanushi in Japan. The American people should know his name. "Yuta Okawa is equal to George Washington. So, from now on, he will spread the new Truth to the United States. You should follow him."

10 Declaring His Rebirth as Donald Trump

Isono And now, you are born as Mr. Donald Trump.

Yuta Okawa Donald Trump.

Washington Oh, yeah.

磯野　では、あなたの秘密ということで。

ワシントン　まあ、いずれにしても、私は国や文明の創始者であり、文明の繁栄期における大物だった。日本の天御中主神と同じ立場にあった。米国民は彼の名前を知らないといかんな。「大川裕太はジョージ・ワシントンに等しいゆえに、これよりのち、彼が新たな真理をアメリカに弘めるであろう。人々よ、彼に従え」。

１０　ドナルド・トランプとしての転生を明言

磯野　現在は、ドナルド・トランプとして生まれていらっしゃると。

大川裕太　ドナルド・トランプですね。

ワシントン　ああ、そうです。

Isono So, you are the next president.

Washington But I'm old. I'm 70 years old, so I don't have enough time. I can only be a president for eight years. You have 50 years until you become my age, so you have enough time.

Yuta Okawa Thank you very much. I need to strive.

Isono OK, once again, could you give a message to the American people?

Washington Americans, please vote for me.

[*Interviewers laugh.*]

Yuta Okawa OK, OK.

Isono Is that all?

磯野　次期大統領ですね。

ワシントン　だが、もうトシだからね。70歳だから、時間が足りない。8年しか大統領をやれない。だが君は、私の年になるまでには、まだ50年あるから、時間は十分あるよ。

大川裕太　ありがとうございます。努力しなければいけませんね。

磯野　はい、もう一度お聞きしますが、米国民にメッセージをいただけますでしょうか。

ワシントン　米国民の皆さん、私に一票をお願いします。

（質問者一同　笑）

大川裕太　はい、分かりました。

磯野　以上でしょうか。

Washington Yeah, that's all…

Isono OK, thank you very…

Washington …and depend on me. Rely on me, rely on me, rely on me.

Yuta Okawa OK.

Washington That's everything.

Isono Everything, OK.

Washington Don't choose Hillary.

Yuta Okawa We respect your message.

Washington It will mean America's death.

Yuta Okawa OK, OK. Thank you very much.

ワシントン　ええ、以上です。

磯野　はい、どうもありがとう……。

ワシントン　それと、私を頼りにしてください。信頼してください。どうか、どうか信頼してください。

大川裕太　はい。

ワシントン　それだけです。

磯野　それだけですね、分かりました。

ワシントン　ヒラリーは選ばないでください。

大川裕太　メッセージは尊重させていただきます。

ワシントン　それは、〝アメリカの死〟を意味する。

大川裕太　はい、はい。ありがとうございました。

Isono Thank you very much for a wonderful lecture.

Washington Thank you. [*Claps once.*]

Ryuho Okawa *Hai* [Japanese word for OK].

Isono Thank you very much, Master Ryuho Okawa.

Ryuho Okawa Hai.

[*Audience applaud.*]

磯野　素晴らしいお話をありがとうございました。

ワシントン　どうもありがとう。(手を一回叩く)

大川隆法　はい。

磯野　大川隆法総裁先生、まことにありがとうございました。

大川隆法　はい。

(会場拍手)

『アメリカ合衆国建国の父
ジョージ・ワシントンの霊言』
大川隆法著作関連書籍

『守護霊インタビュー
ドナルド・トランプ　アメリカ復活への戦略』
　　　　　　　　　　　　　　　　　　（幸福の科学出版刊）
『太陽の法』　　　　　　　　　　　　　　　　（同）
『神秘の法』　　　　　　　　　　　　　　　　（同）

『アメリカ合衆国建国の父
　ジョージ・ワシントンの霊言』

2016年10月19日　初版第1刷

著　者　　大　川　隆　法

発行所　　幸福の科学出版株式会社

〒107-0052　東京都港区赤坂2丁目10番14号
TEL(03) 5573-7700
http://www.irhpress.co.jp/

印刷・製本　　株式会社 堀内印刷所

落丁・乱丁本はおとりかえいたします
©Ryuho Okawa 2016. Printed in Japan. 検印省略
ISBN 978-4-86395-844-9 C0030
Photo：Andrea Izzotti/Shutterstock.com
　　　 /kaktuzoid/Shutterstock.com

大川隆法ベストセラーズ・英語説法&世界の指導者の本心

Power to the Future
未来に力を

英語説法集
日本語訳付き

予断を許さない日本の国防危機。
混迷を極める世界情勢の行方——。
ワールド・ティーチャーが英語で語った、この国と世界の進むべき道とは。

1,400円

キング牧師
天国からのメッセージ
アメリカの課題と夢

英語霊言
日本語訳付き

宗教対立とテロ、人種差別、貧困と移民問題、そして米大統領選のゆくえ——。黒人解放運動に生涯を捧げたキング牧師から現代人へのメッセージ。

1,400円

守護霊インタビュー
ドナルド・トランプ
アメリカ復活への戦略

英語霊言
日本語訳付き

次期アメリカ大統領を狙う不動産王の知られざる素顔とは？ 過激な発言を繰り返しても支持率トップを走る「ドナルド旋風」の秘密に迫る！

1,400円

幸福の科学出版

大川隆法ベストセラーズ・世界の指導者の本心

オバマ大統領の
新・守護霊メッセージ

日中韓問題、TPP交渉、ウクライナ問題、安倍首相への要望……。来日直前のオバマ大統領の本音に迫った、緊急守護霊インタビュー！

英語霊言
日本語訳付き

1,400円

ヒラリー・クリントンの
政治外交リーディング
同盟国から見た日本外交の問題点

竹島、尖閣と続発する日本の領土問題……。国防意識なき同盟国をアメリカはどう見ているのか？ クリントン国務長官の本心に迫る！
【幸福実現党刊】

1,400円

プーチン 日本の政治を叱る

緊急守護霊メッセージ

日本はロシアとの友好を失ってよいのか？ 日露首脳会談の翌日、優柔不断な日本の政治を一刀両断する、プーチン大統領守護霊の「本音トーク」。

1,400円

※表示価格は本体価格（税別）です。

大川隆法「法シリーズ」・最新刊

正義の法
憎しみを超えて、愛を取れ

法シリーズ第22作

テロ事件、中東紛争、中国の軍拡――。
どうすれば世界から争いがなくなるのか。
あらゆる価値観の対立を超える「正義」とは何か。

著者二千冊目となる「法シリーズ」最新刊！

2,000円

第1章　神は沈黙していない――「学問的正義」を超える「真理」とは何か
第2章　宗教と唯物論の相克――人間の魂を設計したのは誰なのか
第3章　正しさからの発展――「正義」の観点から見た「政治と経済」
第4章　正義の原理――「個人における正義」と「国家間における正義」の考え方
第5章　人類史の大転換――日本が世界のリーダーとなるために必要なこと
第6章　神の正義の樹立――今、世界に必要とされる「至高神」の教え

幸福の科学出版

大川隆法シリーズ・最新刊

元自民党幹事長 加藤紘一の霊言
リベラル政治家が考える〝日本の生きる道〟

自民党の要職を歴任してきた〝政界のプリンス〟が、生前の政治家人生、「加藤の乱」の真相、現在の安倍政権、そして過去世の秘密を語る。【幸福実現党刊】

1,400円

凡事徹底と静寂の時間
現代における"禅的生活"のすすめ

目まぐるしい現代社会のなかで、私たちが失ってはいけない大切なことや、智慧を磨き、人格を向上させる"知的エッセンス"が、この一冊に。

1,500円

蓮舫の守護霊霊言
〝民進党イメージ・キャラクター〟の正体

蓮舫氏は果たして総理の器なのか? 国防や外交、天皇制、経済政策についてどう考えるのか? 民進党の人気政治家の驚くべき本音が明らかに。【幸福実現党刊】

1,400円

※表示価格は本体価格(税別)です。

幸福の科学グループのご案内

宗教、教育、政治、出版などの活動を通じて、地球的ユートピアの実現を目指しています。

幸福の科学

1986年に立宗。信仰の対象は、地球系霊団の最高大霊、主エル・カンターレ。世界100カ国以上の国々に信者を持ち、全人類救済という尊い使命のもと、信者は、「愛」と「悟り」と「ユートピア建設」の教えの実践、伝道に励んでいます。

（2016年10月現在）

愛

幸福の科学の「愛」とは、与える愛です。これは、仏教の慈悲や布施の精神と同じことです。信者は、仏法真理をお伝えすることを通して、多くの方に幸福な人生を送っていただくための活動に励んでいます。

悟り

「悟り」とは、自らが仏の子であることを知るということです。教学や精神統一によって心を磨き、智慧を得て悩みを解決すると共に、天使・菩薩の境地を目指し、より多くの人を救える力を身につけていきます。

ユートピア建設

私たち人間は、地上に理想世界を建設するという尊い使命を持って生まれてきています。社会の悪を押しとどめ、善を推し進めるために、信者はさまざまな活動に積極的に参加しています。

海外支援・災害支援

国内外の世界で貧困や災害、心の病で苦しんでいる人々に対しては、現地メンバーや支援団体と連携して、物心両面にわたり、あらゆる手段で手を差し伸べています。

自殺を減らそうキャンペーン

年間約3万人の自殺者を減らすため、全国各地で街頭キャンペーンを展開しています。

公式サイト **www.withyou-hs.net**

ヘレンの会

ヘレン・ケラーを理想として活動する、ハンディキャップを持つ方とボランティアの会です。視聴覚障害者、肢体不自由な方々に仏法真理を学んでいただくための、さまざまなサポートをしています。

公式サイト **www.helen-hs.net**

INFORMATION

お近くの精舎・支部・拠点など、お問い合わせは、こちらまで!
幸福の科学サービスセンター
TEL. **03-5793-1727** (受付時間 火〜金:10〜20時／土・日:10〜18時)
幸福の科学公式サイト **happy-science.jp**

幸福の科学グループの教育・人材養成事業

ハッピー・サイエンス・ユニバーシティ
Happy Science University

ハッピー・サイエンス・ユニバーシティとは

ハッピー・サイエンス・ユニバーシティ(HSU)は、大川隆法総裁が設立された「現代の松下村塾」であり、「日本発の本格私学」です。
建学の精神として「幸福の探究と新文明の創造」を掲げ、
チャレンジ精神にあふれ、新時代を切り拓く人材の輩出を目指します。

学部のご案内

人間幸福学部
人間学を学び、新時代を切り拓くリーダーとなる

経営成功学部
企業や国家の繁栄を実現する、起業家精神あふれる人材となる

未来産業学部
新文明の源流を創造するチャレンジャーとなる

未来創造学部　2016年4月開設
時代を変え、未来を創る主役となる

政治家やジャーナリスト、ライター、俳優・タレントなどのスター、映画監督・脚本家などのクリエーター人材を育てます。 ※

※キャンパスは東京がメインとなり、2年制の短期特進課程も新設します（4年制の1年次は千葉です）。2017年3月までは、赤坂「ユートピア活動推進館」、2017年4月より東京都江東区（東西線東陽町駅近く）の新校舎「HSU未来創造・東京キャンパス」がキャンパスとなります。

住所　〒299-4325　千葉県長生郡長生村一松丙 4427-1
　　　TEL.0475-32-7770

幸福の科学グループの教育・人材養成事業

教育

学校法人 幸福の科学学園

学校法人 幸福の科学学園は、幸福の科学の教育理念のもとにつくられた教育機関です。人間にとって最も大切な宗教教育の導入を通じて精神性を高めながら、ユートピア建設に貢献する人材輩出を目指しています。

幸福の科学学園

中学校・高等学校（那須本校）
2010年4月開校・栃木県那須郡（男女共学・全寮制）
TEL **0287-75-7777**
公式サイト **happy-science.ac.jp**

関西中学校・高等学校（関西校）
2013年4月開校・滋賀県大津市（男女共学・寮及び通学）
TEL **077-573-7774**
公式サイト **kansai.happy-science.ac.jp**

仏法真理塾「サクセスNo.1」 TEL **03-5750-0747**（東京本校）
小・中・高校生が、信仰教育を基礎にしながら、「勉強も『心の修行』」と考えて学んでいます。

不登校児支援スクール「ネバー・マインド」 TEL **03-5750-1741**
心の面からのアプローチを重視して、不登校の子供たちを支援しています。
また、障害児支援の「**ユー・アー・エンゼル！**」運動も行っています。

エンゼルプランV TEL **03-5750-0757**
幼少時からの心の教育を大切にして、信仰をベースにした幼児教育を行っています。

シニア・プラン21 TEL **03-6384-0778**
希望に満ちた生涯現役人生のために、年齢を問わず、多くの方が学んでいます。

NPO 活動支援

学校からのいじめ追放を目指し、さまざまな社会提言をしています。また、各地でのシンポジウムや学校への啓発ポスター掲示等に取り組む一般財団法人「いじめから子供を守ろうネットワーク」を支援しています。

ブログ **blog.mamoro.org**
公式サイト **mamoro.org**
相談窓口 TEL.**03-5719-2170**

幸福の科学グループ事業

政治

幸福実現党

内憂外患(ないゆうがいかん)の国難に立ち向かうべく、2009年5月に幸福実現党を立党しました。創立者である大川隆法党総裁の精神的指導のもと、宗教だけでは解決できない問題に取り組み、幸福を具体化するための力になっています。

幸福実現党 釈量子サイト
shaku-ryoko.net

釈量子@shakuryoko
で検索

党の機関紙
「幸福実現NEWS」

幸福実現党 党員募集中

あなたも幸福を実現する政治に参画しませんか。

○ 幸福実現党の理念と綱領、政策に賛同する18歳以上の方なら、どなたでも党員になることができます。
○ 党員の期間は、党費(年額 一般党員5,000円、学生党員2,000円)を入金された日から1年間となります。

党員になると

党員限定の機関紙が送付されます(学生党員の方にはメールにてお送りします)。
申込書は、下記、幸福実現党公式サイトでダウンロードできます。

住所 〒107-0052
東京都港区赤坂2-10-8 6階
幸福実現党本部

TEL 03-6441-0754
FAX 03-6441-0764
公式サイト hr-party.jp
若者向け政治サイト truthyouth.jp

幸福の科学グループ事業

アー・ユー・ハッピー?
are-you-happy.com

ザ・リバティ
the-liberty.com

幸福の科学出版
TEL 03-5573-7700
公式サイト irhpress.co.jp

出版メディア事業

幸福の科学出版

大川隆法総裁の仏法真理の書を中心に、ビジネス、自己啓発、小説など、さまざまなジャンルの書籍・雑誌を出版しています。他にも、映画事業、文学・学術発展のための振興事業、テレビ・ラジオ番組の提供など、幸福の科学文化を広げる事業を行っています。

ザ・ファクト
マスコミが報道しない「事実」を世界に伝えるネット・オピニオン番組

Youtubeにて随時好評配信中!

ザ・ファクト 検索

ニュースター・プロダクション

ニュースター・プロダクション(株)は、新時代の"美しさ"を創造する芸能プロダクションです。2016年3月には、ニュースター・プロダクション製作映画「天使に"アイム・ファイン"」を公開しました。

公式サイト
newstar-pro.com

入会のご案内

あなたも、幸福の科学に集い、ほんとうの幸福を見つけてみませんか？

幸福の科学では、大川隆法総裁が説く仏法真理をもとに、
「どうすれば幸福になれるのか、また、
他の人を幸福にできるのか」を学び、実践しています。

大川隆法総裁の教えを信じ、学ぼうとする方なら、どなたでも入会できます。入会された方には、『入会版「正心法語」』が授与されます。（入会の奉納は1,000円目安です）

ネットでも入会できます。詳しくは、下記URLへ。
happy-science.jp/joinus

仏弟子としてさらに信仰を深めたい方は、仏・法・僧の三宝への帰依を誓う「三帰誓願式」を受けることができます。三帰誓願者には、『仏説・正心法語』『祈願文①』『祈願文②』『エル・カンターレへの祈り』が授与されます。

三帰誓願

植福の会

植福は、ユートピア建設のために、自分の富を差し出す尊い布施の行為です。布施の機会として、毎月1口1,000円からお申込みいただける、「植福の会」がございます。

ご希望の方には、幸福の科学の小冊子（毎月1回）をお送りいたします。詳しくは、下記の電話番号までお問い合わせください。

月刊「幸福の科学」

ザ・伝道

ヤング・ブッダ

ヘルメス・エンゼルズ

INFORMATION

幸福の科学サービスセンター
TEL. **03-5793-1727** （受付時間 火〜金:10〜20時／土・日:10〜18時）
幸福の科学 公式サイト **happy-science.jp**